From Muhammad to Burj Khalifa:

A Crash Course in 2,000 Years of Middle East History

by

Michael Rank

ISBN 978-148-27722-1-0

Table of Contents

Other Books by Michael Rank
Available on Amazon.com

History's Most Insane Rulers: Lunatics, Eccentrics, and Megalomaniacs From Emperor Caligula to Kim Jong Il, © 2013

History's Worst Dictators: A Short Guide to the Most Brutal Rulers From Emperor Nero to Ivan the Terrible, © 2013

For Melissa and Eleanor

Introduction

My name is Michael Rank, and in this book I am going to describe the entire history of the Middle East, from the beginning of civilization to post-Sept. 11. By the end you will know as much about the Middle East as you would after a year-long university course, sound highly knowledgeable about world affairs to your friends and associates, and learn all this in a just a few minutes a day.

To most Westerners the Middle East appears utterly bewildering. Palestinians want to bomb Israelis that force them at gunpoint to live in restricted parts of the country. Arab leaders are furious about this situation and want Israelis 'wiped off the map' and their land given back to Palestinians, even though the real estate of the Holy Land looks something like rural Utah. And nearly all the world's leaders see fit to chime in on this dispute, even though it's over a chunk of land the size of New Jersey.

Most people understand Israel to be the center stage of the Old Testament, and they understand that there is some kind of connection between the Israel of 4,000 years ago and the Israel of today. But whatever the modern country has in common with the ancient nation of people who walked through the Red Sea is anyone's guess.

To untangle this information and explain it as succinctly as possible, this book is divided into 25 concise chapters. Each one can be read in about five minutes and is devoted to a major theme in Middle East history, such as the beginning of Islam, the Crusades, Genghis Khan, and the beginning of Israel in 1948. To make each chapter clear and practical, each section begins with two statements: the key idea and why it matters to you.

The purpose of this book is not to provide exhaustive information on all cultures and regions of the Middle East; such a work would be larger than the Encyclopedia Britannica. Instead, it aims to give a simple vignette of each topic, assuming that the reader knows little or nothing about them. For those who wish to know more about the topics presented here, they can look at the suggested readings in the back of the book. Those expecting a lengthy discourse of these issues are advised to look at other books, as that is not this author's intent; hence this work being titled a "crash course."

To begin our exploration it is important to understand that in many ways the history of the Middle East isn't that much different from Europe's. Although Middle Easterners share a common culture, they live in countries that are as different from one another as Italy is from Norway. There have been wars fought between these countries that are still a source of bitter disagreement. Many Arabs today resent the fact that they were ruled by the Ottoman Turks for 600 years (we'll get to them later); Turks also resent the fact that the Arabs abandoned them in the face of the British Army during World War I, resulting in the destruction of their empire.

And even though these countries are majority Muslim, the way that they practice and believe their religion is as different as a British Anglican and a Bulgarian Eastern Orthodox Christian. An orthodox Muslim from Saudi Arabia would barely consider an Iranian Shi'a Muslim to be a believer (we'll also get to them later). As we examine the historical developments that created the modern Middle East, for now it's sufficient to remember that the region is full of diverse groups, as different from one another as that of Europeans.

Let us begin our exploration of the Middle East by starting at the best place that anybody can start: the beginning.

Chapter 1:

The Beginning of the Middle East

Key idea: The Middle East has been important throughout world history due to its location at the crossroads of Europe, Asia, and Africa. This is the reason that so many empires in ancient history competed so vigorously for its valuable real estate.

Why this matters to you: After this chapter you will understand how ownership of key land has been at the center of Middle Eastern conflict from the beginning of civilization to the present day.

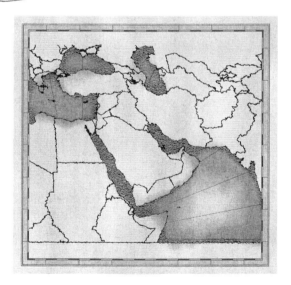

As long as we define "Middle East" as a geographical region, the beginning of Middle East history is synonymous with the beginning of civilization. When most Westerners were in social studies class back in high school, they likely learned about a dizzying array of civilizations such as the Hittites, Sumerians, Akkadians, Phoenicians, and Babylonians. It is highly unlikely that the average person knows or remembers much about these empires, unless they studied archeology or were an Age of Empires aficionado. There's no use in pretending a line of cultural or linguistic continuity linked all these different civilizations, so we are not going to try. But before we skip over the ancient past, one thing worth mentioning is that at least one factor did link these civilizations together: They all destroyed a previous inhabitant of the Middle East and were subsequently destroyed themselves.

Why? Because they inhabited some of the best real estate on the planet. While much of the region from North Africa to modern-day Iran is dry and arid, a swath of fruitful land from the Nile River to the Caspian Sea cuts through this region. Known as the Fertile Crescent, it is the convergence point for Eurasia and Africa for both land and sea. A silk merchant traveling by ship from China to Rome (which could be done even 2,200 years ago) would have to make many stops in the Middle East to stock up on supplies, pay tariffs to local rulers, and secure safe passage over land from the Red Sea to the Mediterranean across Egypt. So if any sort of long-distance trade or military adventures were to take place, it had to involve the Middle East. And if anyone could control this area, then they stood to reap all the profits of these activities, whether

11

through taxing spice merchants or leasing out battle-hardened soldiers to foreign armies.

Long-distance trade first connected the Middle East to the rest of the globe in 3,000 BC, when routes opened up between the Indus Valley in Pakistan and Mesopotamia. For the next five millennia, the Middle East was the center of global activity, until the discovery of the New World altered the flow of commerce and military activity.

It is the value of this real estate that has made the Middle East a dynamic - and highly volatile - place throughout history and up to this day.

Chapter 2:

From the Romans to the Pre-Islamic Period

Key idea: The ancient Middle East and Arabia were a turbulent multi-religious, multi-ethnic society that withstood outside rule because of its harsh climate and mobile people.

Why this matters to you: After this chapter you will understand the key ways that climate and geography can affect and shape a society.

The Middle East was a convergence point between the Roman Empire, the Persian Empire, and the tribes in the desert of Arabia that consisted of a trading confederacy with no ruler. Neither of these empires were ever able to fully control the Arab tribes, nor was any other government. The Roman Empire should have been up to the task, since it could fling troops across the ancient world. If an uprising happened in Germania or unruly raiders were harassing villagers in Armenia, then then the Romans could send soldiers there to end the matter. In fact, one such event was the Jewish uprising against the Romans in 132 AD, known as the Bar Kokhba revolt. Emperor Hadrian sent his general Sextus Julius Severus from Britain to confront this insurrection, and troops came all the way from Germania. Upon arriving in Jerusalem, the army slaughtered 500,000 Jews and deported the rest, where they would live outside the Holy Land until the 1800s when they came to Palestine (causing deep resentment among their new neighbors, which we will get to later).

But armies don't do well in the desert. They need food, supplies, and are only trained to fight soldiers like themselves. And a horseback-mounted desert-dwelling tribesman – like those in Arabia – who can pack up his things quickly in the face of an oncoming army is not in the same danger of being under siege as a rebellious village whose water supply is liable to being cut off or poisoned. In contrast, a desert tribe's lack of cohesion means it likely won't challenge an army head-on, but it also won't be easily conquered. And so it was in Arabia.

The Arabian Peninsula teemed with various religions in Roman times. Christians, Jews, pagans, the fire-worshipping Zoroastrians, and the Manicheans all lived here. Most of these groups in the Middle East and Arabia could be considered religious "losers" from a historical standpoint. By "losers," we mean those people who ended up on the wrong side of history. For Christians this meant those groups whose beliefs were considered heretical by ecumenical councils in the first centuries of Christianity. Nestorians and Monophysites were excommunicated in the 5th century and marginalized by the Eastern Roman Empire. As a result, the Middle East was full of Christians with loose or non-existent ties to the centers of the Christian world in Jerusalem, Constantinople, and Rome, creating a religious

14

vacuum waiting to be filled by a belief structure with a better-defined hierarchy. Therefore it is no great surprise that Islam spread so quickly in this region.

One last geographical point to mention before we discuss the rise of Islam: there is a difference between the Near East and Arabia. When we say the first one, we mean the lands east of the Mediterranean Sea (hence "Near East"). When we say Arabia, we mean the stretches of deserts on the Arabian Peninsula, most of which is now occupied by modern Saudi Arabia and typically forms the backdrop for stock footage of oil rigs overseen by men with checkerboard head coverings and Ray-Ban sunglasses. The cultural difference between these two lands is significant, and the meeting of these two lands produced the hybrid culture known as early Islam.

Near East = east of the Mediterranean Sea

Arabia - Arabian peninsula now S.A, U.A.E, Kwait, Iraq.

Chapter 3:

Muhammed's Early Life and Revelations

Key idea: Muhammed was able to effectively lead a large, diverse populist movement because of, not in spite of, his humble background as an orphaned trader.

Why this matters to you: After this chapter you will understand how Muhammed's early life affected his career as a prophet and leader.

Almost no event has altered the course of history like the rise of Islam, nor did one have such an unlikely beginning. It all started with an illiterate merchant exiled from his tribe working in an obscure corner of the globe. After claiming to receive a prophecy from God, he climbed the social ranks, from an outcast to a local leader and then to the most powerful man in Arabia. After his death, his followers would go on to conquer much of the ancient world in less than a century. Islam now dominates the headlines and is a major source of both unity and tension across the globe, with an estimated 1.2 billion members. What explains its auspicious origin?

It's impossible to say, but the most obvious starting point is the life of Muhammed, the founder of Islam. He was born in 570 A.D. as a member of the Hashimite Clan of the Quarysh Tribe. By the age of two he was an orphan and left in the care of his uncle Abu Talib, a prominent merchant and the leader of the clan. Muhammed grew up traveling in caravans across Arabia, moving from the Mediterranean Sea to the Indian Ocean. These distant travels and contacts with far-flung trade networks would aid him later in life when he set up his own religious and military network that would conquer Arabia and Persia, then North Africa, and eventually press into southern Europe. The following paraphrase from "Mahomet: Founder of Islam," by G.M. Draycott describes the beginning of Muhammed's career:

When Muhammed was 40 he sought solitude more constantly than before and found it at a cave in Mount Hira (known by Muslims today as the *Jebel Nur*, The Mountain of Light). All early Islamic sources say that the angel Gabriel visited him in his sleep with a silken cloth in his hand covered with writing and said to Muhammed, "Read!" "I cannot read," he responded.

Then the angel wrapped the cloth about him and once more commanded, "Read! " Again came the answer, 'I cannot read.' And again the angel covered him, still repeating, "Read!" Then his mouth was opened and he read the first sura of the Qur'an: "Recite thou in the name of thy Lord who created thee." And when he awoke it seemed to him that these words were written on his heart.

Muhammed went immediately up into the mountain, and there Gabriel appeared to him in waking and said: "Thou art God's Prophet, and I am Gabriel." The archangel vanished, but Muhammed remained rooted to the spot until his wife Khadijah's messengers found him and brought him to her.

This event began his career as a prophet. He then went forward and changed the Middle East forever.

Chapter 4:

Muhammed's Preaching and The Expansion of Islam

Key idea: Muhammed is heavily revered in Islam for his life as a prophet, religious leader, teacher, moral example, and mediator of conflict.

Why this matters to you: After this chapter you will understand how the trials of Muhammed's early life enabled him to lead and unite Arabia, then a leaderless and decentralized part of the world.

In 2005 riots broke out across the Muslim world in protest against a Danish newspaper publishing irreverent cartoons of Muhammed. The riots resulted in the torchings and attacks against Danish embassies across the Middle East. In the end over 100 died and over 800 were injured. Why would a drawing of Muhammed prompt such a strong backlash? There are many reasons, but one of them is Muhammed's position as the fulcrum of Islam. To denigrate him is to denigrate the religion. To understand this, let's look further into his story.

According to the Islamic chroniclers, after his visit from Gabriel in 610, Muhammed began receiving prophecies from God. These prophecies formed the core of the Qur'an, which he preached to the residents of Mecca. His teachings focused on the resurrection of the dead, God's judgment against the sinful, his upholding of the righteous, and aspects of right living. However, he also condemned polytheism, which put him out of favor with the Meccan elite, who worshiped multiple gods and also made significant income from pilgrims visiting Mecca's numerous shrines. Despite this opposition he soon gained followers. The first ones were mostly family members and those who had fallen through the cracks in the harsh Arabian nomadic society, in which exile from a tribe or lack of powerful connections meant high susceptibility to an early death.

When Muhammed's wife Khadijah and his uncle Abu Talib (the leader of his clan) died in 619, he lost his protection and the Meccan elite turned on him, leaving him open to extra-tribal assassination from his enemies. He and his followers fled to the city of Medina. When he arrived in the city his skills as an intermediary agent preceded him, and he immediately found a job. The eight tribes of Medina called on Muhammed to mediate conflicts between them, since they had outgrown their eye-for-an-eye judicial system that could that no longer sustain their diverse, cosmopolitan city. In 622 he drafted the Constitution of Medina, creating the first Islamic federation. After this event, conversions to Islam began to occur in larger numbers. The early Medinan converts were also mostly from weak clans that had little recourse to protect themselves.

With Muhammed's power growing, the Meccans confiscated the property of the emigrants. Soon the early Muslims started to raid Meccan caravans loaded with trade goods. The two groups fought numerous battles with each other over the years until 630 when Muhammed and his mostly-Muslim army captured Mecca. By then much of Arabia had converted to Islam.

Muhammed died in 632. Before his death he taught his followers the major tenants of the religion. He also gave a farewell sermon, admonishing his followers not to return to the pre-Islamic practices of polytheism (he also stated that pagans and unbelievers cannot approach the Sacred Mosque, a statement which the Saudi Arabian Grand Mufti used in March 2012 as a pretext to call for all churches in the Arabian peninsula to be bulldozed). Muhammed was buried in Mecca, and today his tomb is part of the pilgrimage route that all Muslims are required to make at least once in their lives.

Muhammed has left an indelible mark on Islam. The Five Pillars of Islam either directly reference him or were handed down by him. First, any new convert must recite the *Shahadah* (Profession of Faith) that "there is no god except Allah and Muhammed is the Messenger of Allah." Second, Muslims must attend five daily prayers, which are announced across the Muslim world from mosque loudspeakers that also repeat the *Shahadah*. Third, Muslims must give 2.5% of their wealth to the poor. Fourth, Muslims must fast during the month of Ramadan (the month the Qur'an was revealed to Muhammed) and abstain from eating, drinking, and sex from sunrise to sunset for 30 days. Last, they must go on the pilgrimage to Mecca.

In his lifetime Muhammed transformed the Arabian Peninsula. In the following chapters we will see that in less than three generations his followers would transform the ancient world.

Chapter 5:

The Qur'an

Key idea: Muslims revere the Qur'an more than Christians do the Bible or Jews the Torah; they almost esteem it to the level that Christians do Jesus.

Why this matters to you: After this chapter you will understand the place of respect and authority that the Qur'an holds in Islam and the reason that Muslims have rioted in response to desecrations of this book throughout the last decade.

In 2005, Newsweek magazine claimed that a guard at Guantanamo Bay flushed a Qur'an down a toilet.

Less than a week later, protestors in Afghanistan were chanting death threats against the U.S. and burning American flags. The protests left 15 dead and 100 injured. The story later turned out to be false, but similar protests for supposed desecrations of the Qur'an have happened over the years, with the most recent episode in Afghanistan against U.S. soldiers who accidentally burned hundreds of Qur'ans in February 2012 as part of destroying the personal effects of Afghani prisoners. Why would the soiling of one book push so many people to such rage?

Because the importance of the Qur'an to Muslims is in a category all its own, beyond the Bible to Christians and the Torah to Jews. Christians believe that God communicated through humans to share his message with humanity; Muslims believe the Qur'an is the literal word of God that existed in its entirety for all eternity. For this reason, most Muslim scholars claim that a Qur'an cannot be translated from Arabic into another language the way that Greek and Hebrew manuscripts have been translated into the Bible. As the Qur'an is the perfect revelation of God, a translated Qur'an is no Qur'an at all and merely an "interpretation."

Muslims claim that the Qur'an came down to humans through a series of revelations that the angel Gabriel gave to Muhammed, starting in 610 at a cave near Mecca. His followers memorized these fragments, and they were later compiled into a book a few decades later by the third Ummayad Caliph 'Uthman. They say that although

Muhammed was illiterate, his ability to narrate such a work is proof of its divine origin.

The Qur'an is divided into suras, which are much like books of the Bible. It is a bit confusing to read for the uninitiated, as the suras are arranged from the longest to shortest books, not by chronology. The verses are separated into two groups: the Meccan Suras and the Medina Suras. The Meccan Suras were written before the military growth of Islam, when Muslims were not in a position of power and were under pressure to accommodate multiple religious beliefs. It is these verses that often speak of love and tolerance of other religions. The later-written Medina Suras came at a time when Muslims had gained power. Here much less tolerance and accommodation is shown to other religions.

Superstition about the Qur'an abounds in Islam's history, much like the Bible did for Christians. In the 1500s, European diplomats who traveled to Turkey reported that while lodging at travelers' inns they noticed a strange sight: The bricks and stones that made up the walls had hundreds of pieces of paper stuck in the cracks. The Hapsburg diplomat Ogier Ghiselin de Busbecq asked an innkeeper about these curious scraps of paper and the paradoxically powerful effect they had on the tenants, since nearly all of them were illiterate. The innkeeper responded that the tenants were afraid these scraps could have Qur'anic verses written on them. And to throw away such holy writings would be to invite a curse upon their head on judgment day:

"On the day of the last judgment, when Mahomet will summon his followers from purgatory to heaven and eternal bliss, the only road open to them will be over a red-hot gridiron, which they must walk across with bare feet. A painful ordeal methinks. Picture to yourself a cock skipping and hopping over hot coals! Now comes the marvel. All the paper they have preserved from being trodden on and insulted, will appear unexpectedly, stick itself under their feet, and be of the greatest service in protecting them from the red-hot iron. This great boon awaits those who save paper from bad treatment. On some occasions our guides were most indignant with my servants for using paper for some very dirty work, and reported it to me as an outrageous offense. I replied that they must not be surprised at such acts on the part of my servants. What could they expect, I added, from people who are accustomed to eat pork?"

-- The Turkish Letters of Ogier de Busbecq (1522-1592)

Chapter 6:

The Split Into Sunnis and Shias

Key idea: The conflict between Islam's two major sects - Sunni and Shia - has lasted for over 1,300 years and started with a war over control of the Caliphate.

Why this matters to you: After this chapter you will understand the diversity of belief in Islam and be able to make sense of the violent conflicts between Muslims in places like Iraq and Lebanon.

What is the difference between a Sunni Muslim and Shiite Muslim? If you don't know the answer then don't feel guilty - members of Congress, FBI officials, and counter-terrorism experts were asked this same question in 2006, and few could answer correctly. While the answer seems only important to Trivial Pursuit masters, understanding the differences is key to making sense of the constant infighting that takes place in the Middle East between Muslim groups (notable cases include the Iran-Iraq war of 1980-1988, the former nation being Shiite and the latter Sunni, and the Iraqi insurgency in the late 2000s).

The origin of the split comes from the expansion of Islam. As Islam spread from Baghdad to France over a 100-year period, differences started to appear between Muslim groups, much like the split in Christianity between Catholics, Eastern Orthodox Christians and Protestants. After the death of Muhammed, the Muslim community chose a replacement as the leader of their religion. This person would be known as the Caliph ("successor" or "representative" in Arabic) and the domain of his leadership was known as the Caliphate. Like the pope of the Middle Ages, the Caliph maintained both spiritual and political power over his subjects. But unlike the pope, the Caliph was recognized as the universal head of his religion for only a few decades before the community split.

The first Caliph was Abu Bakr (632-634). He was among the first converts to Islam, and the father-in-law to Muhammed, who married his daughter A'ishah. The second was Omar (634-644), who led Muslim armies against the Byzantine Empire to the north and completely enveloped the Persian Empire in 636, which had existed for a thousand years. The third Caliph was 'Uthman (644-656). Under his reign the Caliphate expanded to encompass regions extending from Armenia to Algeria. He was also responsible for collecting the prophecies of Muhammed and compiling them into one book: The Qur'an. But he was not without dissenters. Many thought that 'Uthman had given an unfair proportion of the spoils of war to his own tribe. Consequently, he was assassinated by rebels and the reign of Ali, the Fourth Caliph, began.

The conflict between the tribes loyal to 'Uthman (which became the Ummayads) and the tribes loyal to Ali led to an all-out civil war in 657.

The two groups ultimately declared a truce, but Ali's followers were so angered with him for doing so that they assassinated him. The followers of Ali may have killed their leader but they were still loyal to his cause and felt marginalized by the Ummayads. Ali's sons Hassan and Hussein staged another battle against the Ummayads in 680 in Iraq. Hussein was killed and his martyrdom is central to the Shiite movement (pictures of him usually appear at protest rallies in Iran today).

The split between these two groups resulted in a 1,400-year division between Sunnis and Shias that persists to this day. Cultural differences have sprung up between them over the centuries. For example, Shiite boys are often named Ali or Hassan, while the names Omar, 'Uthman, or Abu Bakar are popular with Sunnis. Additionally, some ultra-orthodox Shias will whip themselves on the holiday of Ashura to commemorate the deaths of Hassan and Hussein.

These differences even affect how these groups dress. While your average Sunni and Shia look quite a bit alike, a pious Shia Muslim doesn't wear a necktie (Iran's bombastic prime minister Mahmoud Ahmadinejad never wears one in public) while an equally pious Sunni will sport a long beard.

Chapter 7:

The Golden Age of Islam:
The Abbasid Empire

Key idea: In the Middle Ages the Middle East was the world's center for scholarship, culture, and science as Europe had barely emerged from the Dark Ages.

Why this matters to you: After this chapter you will understand how scientific golden ages come about, and why one such period occurred in the Middle East while Europe was in the Dark Ages.

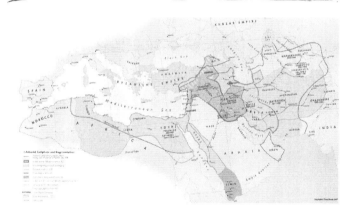

"The ink of a scholar is more holy that the blood of a martyr." So goes the hadith, a saying of Islam ascribed to Muhammed, which is an apt description of the Abbasid period (750-1258). The 9th and 10th centuries especially are considered by many historians to be the cultural and scientific golden age of Islam.

From 661-750 the leaders of the Islamic world were the Ummayad Caliphate. They were the winners in the first civil war in Islam and centered the capital of the Islamic world in Syria. However, many Muslims resented that the Umayyad family showed favoritism to its own clans and did not descend from Muhammad's family. The Abbasid family, which claimed direct descent from Muhammad and therefore had a stronger basis of legitimacy, appealed to groups marginalized by the Ummayads and overthrew them in 750. From this moment they began a five-hundred year reign and established their capital of Baghdad as the global center of learning and scholarship.

Baghdad sat at the crossroads of Eurasia and regained its status as the world's center for philosophy, science, and medicine (as it also held this title during the Assyrian and Babylonian Empires). Many texts from the ancient world were assembled and translated into Arabic at the House of Wisdom, the world's first scientific venture. Were it not for this endeavor, texts written in ancient Greek and other languages would have, most likely been lost. Philosophy and science were discovered, rediscovered and promulgated during this time, including Aristotelian philosophy, geometry, algebra (an Arabic word in origin), and the algorithm (also an Arabic word). Early forms of the scientific method were developed and eventually spread to Europe, an event many scholars believe planted the seeds of the Renaissance. The Abbasids also had a long-lasting influence on the Islamic world, as they were the first to develop elaborate bureaucracies. Within this framework, classes of religious scholars known as ulema coalesced and hammered out Sunni orthodoxy as it is understood today.

The Abbasid's power started to wane as other Muslim groups challenged their authority. Such groups included the Ghaznavids, a dynasty founded by former soldier-slaves that extended all the way to India; and the Seljuks, a Turkish and Persian Sunni Muslim dynasty that ruled much of the Middle East and Central Asia from the 11th to 14th centuries.

However, the final death blow to the Abbasid Caliphate was brought about by a group that no one expected. It wasn't a rival Middle Eastern Muslim state or the Christian Byzantine Empire. Rather it was an ethnic group on the outskirts of Muslim and Chinese civilization that was at best ignored by other empires but mostly seen as a troublesome nuisance for its raids and attacks on villagers. But this group would rise to power in the 13th century and be led by a dynamic warrior that would plunder Asia and alter the world map. His name was Genghis Khan and he led the Mongol Horde.

Chapter 8:

The Crusades

Key idea: The Catholic Church mounted multiple military campaigns against Middle Eastern Islamic states to recapture Jerusalem (1195-1291). The crusaders ultimately failed in their objective, but they did leave the legacy of a deeper connection between the Middle East and Europe.

Why this matters to you: After this chapter you will understand how inter-religious wars are triggered and why the Crusades remain so vivid in European and Middle Eastern memory to this day.

While European Christians had been aware of the spread of Islam since its earliest centuries, the fact was generally regarded by these rulers with passivity. This would change in the 11th century when Europe received a powerful wake-up call. In 1071 at the battle of Manzikert, the Seljuk Turks, a Central Asian empire whose capital was in Iran, destroyed the Byzantine Empire's army and flooded into Asia Minor, which is modern-day Turkey. The Seljuks almost conquered Constantinople, then the most magnificent Christian city on earth. Byzantine Emperor Alexios I appealed to Pope Urban II to send him mercenaries to push back the advances of the Turks.

Christians were also scandalized by the destruction of holy sites in Jerusalem, which had been a site of pilgrimage since the fourth century. In particular, in 1009 the Fatimid Caliph's destruction of the Holy Sepulchre Church in Jerusalem, believed to be built at the site of Jesus' crucifixion, provoked the church into action. In 1095 Pope Urban II called for a religious expeditionary war to reclaim Jerusalem for Christendom. He proclaimed that the campaign would serve as penance for all who took part, whether knight or commoner. Additionally, participants were told they would have the opportunity to acquire homes in Palestine. With much of Europe enduring starvation conditions at the time, hundreds of thousands answered the call.

The First Crusades were a success, and the armies established four kingdoms near or along the Mediterranean coast, including one in Jerusalem. But whatever holy objectives launched the crusades, its aims quickly veered off course. In 1099, with the capture of Jerusalem, the crusading armies massacred 70,000 Jewish and Muslim men, women and children in the city. Defeats followed in subsequent crusades, as when the Seljuks reconquered the town of Edessa in south-central Anatolia. And in 1187 the famed 'Ayyubid leader Saladin recaptured Jerusalem. Upon hearing the news, Pope Urban III died of a heart attack.

By 1202 the Fourth Crusade started, which was a complete disaster for Christendom. Pope Innocent II called on Christian armies to invade the Holy Land through Egypt, but since many ships were needed, Venice was contracted out to ferry the troops. It was an enormously lucrative contract for Venice; they received 85,000 marks of silver, a war profiteering amount that would make Halliburton blush. In 1204 the Crusaders lost sight of their mission to fight in the Holy Land and laid siege to the Eastern Orthodox city of Constantinople, occupying it for 60 years and causing massive devastation. The Byzantine empire was hobbled, and it would never recover, being completely conquered by the Ottoman Turks in 1453.

The last crusader kingdom in the Holy Land of Acre fell in 1291. The legacy of the Crusades left bitter relations between Christians and Muslims and between Latin Catholics and Greek Orthodox in Byzantium. As a result some Christians preferred to be ruled by Muslims instead of other Christian denominations that had exploited them in the past. In the 1300s, when the Turkish Ottoman Empire began conquering Eastern Orthodox Christian villages that were under Catholic control, some Orthodox Christians commented that they preferred the sultan's turban to the cardinal's hat.

But the encounters between these groups were not altogether negative. The crusaders brought back with them to Europe such technology as the windmill and new techniques for forging weapons. Trade and the flow of information also increased as maritime trading colonies grew in Italy, cities that would be key in the Renaissance.

Nevertheless, the legacy of the Crusades is mostly a negative one between Muslims and Christians with the wound remaining unhealed to this day. Some Christians consider the wars as a counter-attack in the face of centuries of Muslims hostilities, while Muslims think of them as the first stage in a vast plan of exploitation of the Middle East that would culminate in European colonialism of the 1800s. But as the previous paragraph shows, even in the most ostensibly violent times of Middle Eastern history, positive effects could still result from the inter-cultural encounter.

Chapter 9:

Muslims and Their Rule over Christians and Jews

Key idea: Muslim treatment of Christian and Jewish subjects has been a mixed bag in history. Although Muslims didn't give anything like free expression of religion, in the Middle Ages a Christian or Jew had a better life under Muslim rule than vice versa.

Why this matters to you: After this chapter you will understand how to make sense of the rights of religious minorities today by understanding their situation in the past.

In April 2011 the Organization of the Islamic Conference (OIC) - an umbrella group for 57 Muslim nations - issued a report recommending that the incitement of religious hatred be criminalized. The report made no mention of Christianity and Judaism but singled out Islam as a unique recipient of longstanding religious discrimination, citing such recent events as the 2006 Danish cartoons that mocked Muhammed, or Pastor Terry Jones' 2011 burning of a Qur'an. They and other Muslim rights groups have claimed that Muslims have always treated other religions with respect. In contrast, critics such as Robert Spencer argue that throughout history Islam has been the one to impose itself in a totalitarian fashion onto other religions. They assert that wherever Islam has spread it made free worship for other religions impossible. Which version is correct?

In a sense, both are correct and neither is correct. It is true that the Islamic regimes of the medieval period never promoted anything like a Jeffersonian concept of individual liberty among their subjects. In 717 AD the Umayyad Caliph Omar II issued a mandate to Christians living on conquered lands: They could choose to convert to Islam, pay a poll tax, or be killed. Christians were also routinely enslaved and subjected to the confiscation of their property. In Islamic courts their testimony would only be worth a fraction of a Muslim's. And the permission to build new churches or synagogues was dependent on the generosity of the Muslim ruler at the time.

And yet often times Christians and Jews enjoyed better lives under Muslim rule than vice-versa. Keep in mind that these events occurred in the Middle Ages, a time when nobody had the constitutional assurance of life, liberty, and the pursuit of happiness. Taken in historical context, it is noteworthy that in Muslim states, Christians and Jews had a social space carved out for them. Throughout much of history, most Muslim leaders were far less interested in harassing their non-Muslim subjects than collecting their tax money.

The Ottoman Empire's economy mostly depended on the collection of a non-Muslim poll tax. When the Ottoman Sultan Selim I (r. 1512-1520) wanted to convert all his Christian subjects to Islam, his advisers ruled out the idea because a

38

majority of their revenue came from the Christian poll tax. Indeed, when Jews fled Spain in the late 1400s during the Spanish Inquisition, many of them made for the Ottoman Empire, where they were well received. Their descendents still live in Turkey, and in some parts of Istanbul one can hear Ladino, a Hebrew-inflected form of Spanish.

In the modern era, Muslim nations have generally established a poor track record of protecting religious minorities. A 2012 Religious Freedom report ranks nearly all Muslim countries as "Partly Free" or "Unfree." Attempted Muslim terrorist attacks in the United States and Europe are often accompanied by statements from the attacker justifying their actions by commands from the Qur'an demanding all Muslims to engage in holy war (jihad) against non-Muslims. In 1998, Osama bin Laden declared an open-ended jihad against the entire Western World, which became the rallying cry for al-Qaeda. In response to these trends, Christians and Jews in the Middle East have engaged in a mass exodus from Muslim-dominated countries for decades.

Yet, as is often the case, the historical record is more diverse and complex than current events are made to suggest. As Muslim immigration to Europe and America increases each year (approximately 50 million Muslims live in Europe, and according to some recent accounts the Muslim population has surpassed the Jewish numbers in America) perhaps there are some lessons about inter-religious harmony to be taken from the past.

Chapter 10:

The Wrath of Khan:
The Mongol Invasion

Key idea: Genghis Khan rose from an obscure corner of the globe to create the world's largest empire, stretching from China to Eastern Europe. He is still revered in much of the Middle East and Central Asia as a great conqueror.

Why this matters to you: After this chapter you will understand how Genghis Khan shaped our modern world and how he has come to hold such a tremendous place of prestige in the Middle East, despite the fact that he was not a Muslim.

One of the most influential men in Islamic history was not even a Muslim. His name was Chingiz Khan (Genghis Khan to you and me) and he emerged from a forgotten corner of the Eurasian Steppe and formed an army that plundered the greatest kingdoms and empires of the time. The empire he created, and that his descendents extended, was the largest contiguous empire in world history. Its vassals included Korea, China, the Middle East, Russia, the Caucasus, and Eastern Europe.

Genghis Khan was born in 1162 in Mongolia and practiced the shamanist religion of medieval Central Asia. Although he had Buddhists, Muslims, and even Christians in his court, he and his sons maintained their practice of shamanism. In 1258 his grandson Hulagu Khan reached the Abbasid Empire and destroyed the Caliphate in Baghdad, an event as devastating to Islam as if an army had ransacked Rome, killed the pope, and razed the Vatican to the ground, never to be rebuilt. The Middle East that Hulagu encountered was an empire being ripped apart at the margins by break-away states and upstart rival leaders; the Middle East he left behind had no central religious authority, creating a power vacuum for centuries.

As he began to gather soldiers around him, Genghis Khan diverted from Mongol tradition in two ways that would lead to his world empire. First, he did not assign duties and honor based on family relations and kinship networks but ability and loyalty, a major innovation in a land where blood relations were typically all that stood between a person and death. The promise of future spoils of war to his soldiers quickly attracted many to his rule (a common motif for Muslim and Christian rulers in the Middle Ages). Second, he absorbed disparate elements of society into his rule. After conquering a village, rather than chasing off soldiers and abandoning the women and children, he absorbed them into his nascent empire. This flexibility made for a mobile empire of thousands of horseback-mounted soldiers who could quickly conquer, incorporate the elements of the conquered place into their domain, and keep expanding.

The positive legacy of Genghis Khan was the unification of his domains, which created peace across much of Eurasia, a time known as the 'Pax Mongolica.' This also allowed open trade along the Silk Road and connected Southeast Asia to Central Europe. This was the route taken by Marco Polo, when from 1271 to 1295, he traveled overland from Italy to the court of Kublai Khan, Ghengis' grandson.

Despite the fact that he and his descendents decimated the Middle East, Ghengis Khan is still respected by Muslims today as a world conqueror. Ghengis remains a popular boy's name in Turkey and other Central Asian countries, and he is a favored mascot of Middle Eastern restaurants. He even occupies a special place in Islamic history and is considered a true world conqueror blessed by God and matched only by Alexander the Great and Timur the Tatar, who conquered much of Central Asia in the 1400s. In the Middle Ages, countless Muslim rulers vied to match Ghengis Khan's conquests, hoping that such action would show they were appointed by God to conquer the world and usher in the end times.

Genghis was also a popular man with the ladies, producing countless children through his many wives and concubines. Recently an international team of geneticists announced after a 10-year survey that one out of every 200 men on earth are directly descended from Genghis Khan; in the the domains of the former Mongolian Empire that number rises to one in eight. He fathered countless children through wives and concubines, his oldest son had 40 legitimate sons, and his grandson Kublai Khan had 22 sons. His sons and grandsons were prominent Middle Eastern and Central Asian rulers in their own right, and their descendents could immediately claim prestige as a ruler by showing their connection to Genghis.

You could say there's a little bit of Genghis in all of us.

Chapter 11:

The Middle East in Europe: The Ottoman Empire (1516-1918)

Key idea: The Turkish Ottoman Empire controlled all the Middle East and a third of Europe for 400 years, connecting East and West.

Why this matters to you: After this chapter you will understand East-West interactions in the recent past and the political events that created the modern Middle East.

When you hear the word "Ottoman" today the first image that likely comes to mind is an overstuffed footrest accompanied by a luxury sofa or recliner purchased from a furniture outlet. "Why would an empire take its name from an article of furniture?" you may wonder. It turns out it is the empire that is the namesake of the furniture: In the 1800s overstuffed furniture designed with an Oriental motif was popular in Europe and known as ala Turca furniture, or "Ottoman." Footstools aside, the Ottoman Empire was the dominant Muslim power after the Middle Ages, controlling the Middle East and much of Southeast Europe for centuries.

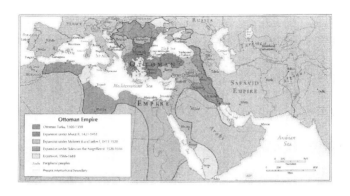

It surprises many people to learn that the predominant power in the Middle East for hundreds of years were the Turks, not Arabs. At the time the Turks would have likely been equally as surprised. They did not have the same cultural resume as the Arabs or Persians, who claimed to have inherited the pedigree of past Near Eastern civilizations. In contrast they originated in Central Asia and first encountered Islam as it expanded out from the Middle East. Arab armies enslaved the shamanistic Turkic soldiers for their fearsome martial skills and ability to shoot moving targets from horseback at full gallop.

In 1300 a Turkish chieftain named Osman formed a principality in northwestern Anatolia (today's Turkey). He conquered only a few towns in his lifetime, but his sons would go on to conquer fortresses, then cities, then major armies. The snowball effect of these conquests continued for seven generations, until 1453, when his descendent Mehmet conquered Constantinople, the capital of the Eastern Roman Empire. Mehmet's grandson Selim I would expand his victories and conquer the Middle East in 1516-7, taking control of Egypt, Jerusalem, and the holy cities of Mecca and Medina. His son Suleyman the Magnificent, the tenth Ottoman Sultan, turned his sights toward Europe. He pushed far into the West and conquered Hungary, which the Ottomans would control for 150 years. Suleyman even reached the gates of Vienna in 1526 and boasted that he would soon capture it before moving on to Rome. The siege failed, but the thought of a Turkish conquest of Europe haunted many European monarchs for the next two centuries. The great reformer Martin Luther even worried that God was using the Turks to punish Europe for sins committed by the papacy. This anxiety continued until the Europeans begun to push back the Turks in 1699.

The Ottoman Empire shrank throughout the 1700s and 1800s in the face of European military gains, the rise of Russia, and the spread of Western technologies such as the steam ship, telegraph, and modern manufacturing. In response, the Ottomans saw their share of international trade plummet as merchants bypassed their Middle Eastern land routes in favor of using ships to reach the New World. The Ottoman Empire attempted to reform its laws by introducing equal rights for all subjects regardless of religion, but these attempts came too late. By the end of 19th century, it had become clear that the Ottoman Empire would not be long for this world. The European chattering class referred to it as the "Sick Man of Europe" and believed the Ottoman Empire would soon be ripe for colonizing by European nations, which by the end of the 19th century controlled 80 percent of the globe. These competing Ottoman and European visions would finally clash in the First World War, the event that created the modern Middle East.

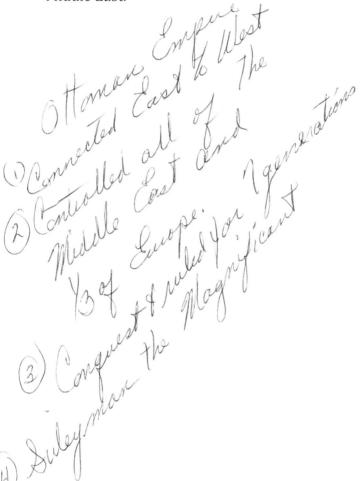

Ottoman Empire

1) Connected East to West

2) Controlled all of The Middle East and 1/3 of Europe. 7 generations

3) Conquest & ruled for

4) Suleyman the Magnificent

Chapter 12:

World War 1: The Creation of The Modern Middle East

Key idea: The Middle East was reformed into its modern condition by British and French officials after its political collapse in World War I.

Why this matters to you: After this chapter you will understand how the modern Middle East was created and why many Middle Easterners distrust Western nations to this day.

As World War I approached, the colonial powers of Europe could see that the Ottoman Empire was on the verge of collapse and that its vast Middle East holdings - from modern-day Turkey to the southern tip of the Arabian Peninsula - would soon be up for grabs, making for lucrative new colonies. When the Ottomans entered World War I on the side of the Germans, it was a decision that ultimately doomed the empire.

The British and French knew this and sent agents and armies into the Middle East to foment unrest. In 1916 they drew up a secret plan called the Sykes-Picot Agreement. It determined how the Ottoman territories would be divided: France would obtain Lebanon, Syria, and southern Turkey; Britain the states in the Arabian Peninsula and Palestine, even though the British had promised the Arabs independence in return for their military support against the Turks during the war. The two nations would also make Jerusalem a city under international protection and a refuge area for Jews. Later the League of Nations agreed to the establishment of a mandate system of French and British control. Following the Ottoman defeat in 1918 (and its total collapse in 1923), this is exactly what happened.

After the war, the borders of the modern Middle East emerged. They were sometimes arbitrarily drawn and not based on national history, geographical features, or the opinions of the inhabitants. Winston Churchill, then Britain's colonial secretary, drew up the plans for Iraq, a Frankenstein-like amalgamation of three Ottoman provinces whose inhabitants - Kurds in the North, Sunni Muslims in the center, Shias in the South, and various other religious and ethnic groups sprinkled in - had very little in common. This is part of the reason for the internal violence during the insurgency after the 2003 US invasion left no dictator to force "peace" on the population by draconian measures. British and French influence remained in the Middle East until World War II. In response, Arab nationalism began at this time, as did political Islam.

Today the legacy of World War I is alive and well in the Middle East. Many citizens and politicians are suspicious that Western actions seek to exploit the land and natural resources. While some of these suspicions fall into the realm of bizarre conspiracy theory (one idea posited during the US invasion of Iraq was that America was acting to colonize the Middle East because of their knowledge of an impending asteroid collision with North America slated to occur in 2030), they clearly have historical precedent for these ideas. After all, it was European political actions during World War I that created an entity despised by many people in the Middle East: The state of Israel.

Chapter 13:

The Beginning of Israel

Key idea: Most Jews lived outside modern day Israel for thousands of years until they started to return there in the 1800s due to the influential ideas of Theodor Herzl, the founder of Zionism.

Why this matters to you: After this chapter you will understand what connects ancient and modern Israel, and to be aware of the unifying ideology of Israel today.

Israel is both ancient and new. The ancient version as described in the Bible is almost 4,000 years old and witnessed the rise and fall of empires that today only exist in high school history books. The new version is barely 60 years old and an invention of the modern era. How could a nation of Jews, the world's oldest monotheistic religion, be an invention of the modern era? Well, believe it or not, it all has to do with the media.

The intellectual father of modern Israel was a Jewish journalist named Theodor Herzl (pictured). Born in Budapest, Hungary and working as a foreign correspondent in Constantinople and London, Herzl reported extensively on the political and cultural events of 19th-century Europe. He was alarmed at the growing anti-Semitism in Europe and Russia, as scientists placed Jews at the bottom of racial pyramids (with Caucasian races on top, of course) and opportunistic politicians appropriated this research to blame Jews for social problems and push anti-Semitic policies, such as the Russian pogroms in the 1880s. Herzl believed that Jews could no longer live safely as religious minorities sprinkled throughout multiple nations. They had to group together for mutual safety.

At the first Zionist congresses in the 20th century, several locations were floated as a possible Jewish homeland since few Jews had actually lived in Israel since the Bar Kokhba revolt against the Romans in 132 AD (see Chapter 2).

Some suggested Madagascar, Uganda, or Far Eastern Russia. But in the end, they couldn't resist their ancestral homeland. The geographical dimensions of biblical Israel were even described in the Old Testament, adding historical and cultural precedent to re-settling the region. Furthermore, Israel seemed open for settlement at the time, having been the province of Palestine under the Ottoman Empire for the last four hundred years, a relatively unimportant political unit to the Sultan and his bureaucracy thousands of miles away in Istanbul. Thus began the first major influx of Jewish migrants to the Middle East following the initial wave of Russian Jews from the pogroms of the 1880s.

Chapter 14:

Waves of Jewish Migrants (1880s-1950s)

Key idea: The population of Palestine shifted from Arab Muslim to Jewish following waves of Jewish immigrants, most of whom fled persecution in Europe, the Middle East, and Russia.

Why this matters to you: After this chapter you will understand how the demographics of the Middle East have shifted so dramatically, and why Jews have flocked to a place surrounded by unfriendly neighbors.

One hundred years ago there was barely one Jew for every 100 Muslims in modern-day Israel. By 1918 the number jumped to one in 10, and by 1948 the population was roughly even. What caused such an abrupt demographic shift? It was a massive influx of Jews that was too large-scale and haphazard to be centrally planned, along with the emigration and deportation of Muslim inhabitants.

When Jews first began to arrive in Israel in the late nineteenth century, they didn't imagine that the end result would be an independent nation. Instead, they hoped to occupy a semi-autonomous region under the umbrella of the Ottoman Muslim Turks (which had housed Jews escaping the Spanish Inquisition 400 years earlier). Theodor

Herzl even personally petitioned Sultan Abdulhamit II for this request and was flat-out rejected. Ironically, what Herzl and other Jewish leaders couldn't accomplish in bringing Jews to Palestine would be achieved by rising Anti-Semitism. As Jews throughout Eastern Europe fled their homelands many went to America, but a few others came to Israel.

The first immigrants escaped Russian and Eastern European pogroms. They considered immigrating to Israel a tenant of Zionist ideology and described the act of returning to their homeland with Hebrew word Aliyah ("ascent"). In the First Aliyah between 1882 and 1903, nearly 35,000 Jews arrived in Ottoman Syria and established agricultural communities. Eighty thousand more arrived from Russia in the Second and Third Aliyahs from 1904 to 1923, particularly after World War I. Israel's Jewish population saw its sharpest spike with the Fourth and Fifth Aliyahs as Jews escaped growing anti-Semitism in Hungary, Poland, and Germany. A total of 350,000 arrived, with half that number arriving from 1933-1936.

Other Jews who survived the Holocaust came after the end of World War II. Eventually, the anti-Jewish sentiment of Europe made its way to the Middle East where it created enough unrest to compel Jews from communities which had existed in Arab countries for thousands of years to leave their homes for a new homeland. From the post-WW II period to the early 1970s, around 900,000 Jews left Arab lands through immigration or expulsion. The whirlwind of 20th-century Jewish resettlement lasted for six decades but ultimately resulted in the creation of a Jewish homeland.

Balfour Declaration 1917

British mandate for Palestine

Chapter 15:

The Road to Israel's Formation (1917-1948)

Key idea: Israel became a state due to British support for a Jewish homeland. The British tried to mediate peace between Jews and Muslims in Palestine but failed.

Why this matters to you: After this chapter you will understand the history of Israel's relationship with the West and why many Middle Easterners think Western support for Israel comes at their expense.

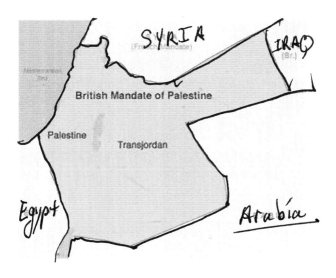

Following the defeat of the Ottoman empire, the advent of British control over Palestine in 1917 marked the first time since the crusades in 1191 that a non-Muslim power controlled Jerusalem. As they administered it for the next three decades, many British politicians noticed the immigration of Jews to Palestine and looked favorably on the Zionist movement. They supported the creation of a Jewish homeland, but with an important caveat - they did not want to compromise the moral and material well-being of the Muslim inhabitants there. How they were supposed to do that was anyone's guess. And it has been anyone's guess for at least the last nine decades.

The backbone of British diplomatic support for a Jewish state was the 1917 Balfour Declaration, in which British Foreign Secretary Lord Balfour declared to Britain's Jewish community his government's support of the creation of a Jewish national homeland in Palestine. In 1920 Britain created and administered a state carved out of Ottoman Syria, part of which consisted of Palestine (modern-day Israel). It was known as the British Mandate for Palestine, and the League of Nations consented that Britain oversee the area until it could function as a self-sustaining nation.

Many Arabs were unhappy with these developments, feeling betrayed that the British had not given them an independent homeland as the British High Commissioner in Egypt had promised in 1915. As a result, the Arab leadership refused to participate in any institution that included Jewish leadership, making the development of a Jewish-Arab Palestinian state enormously difficult. Tensions within Arab communities continued to rise with the tide of Jewish immigrants arriving from Europe and Russia. Coupled with a sense that they were losing control of their homeland, this tension reached a threshold in 1920 and 1921 with Arab riots breaking out in response to evictions caused by the Jewish purchase of land.

When Hitler took power in 1933, Jews flooded into Palestine. The demographic upset and the British killing of Palestinian militia leader Sheikh Izz ad-Din al-Qassam led to the Arab revolts of 1936-1939. The British supported Jewish auxiliaries, and it was ultimately successful. In total 5,000 Arabs died (another 10,000 were injured) and 400 Jews died. Following this conflict, the British became convinced that Jews and Arabs could not co-exist and that partition of the land was necessary. But first the British decided to stymie the effects of further Jewish immigration. In 1939 they limited the number of Jewish arrivals to a quota of 15,000 annually for the next five years. Due to the ongoing Holocaust, far more than this attempted to enter Palestine per annum. The British placed those that exceeded the 15,000 into detention camps, an action which created a permanent rift between the British and Jewish leadership. Following World War II, 250,000 Jews were in displaced person camps in Europe, hoping to enter Israel, but Britain refused to alter the quota.

This refusal resulted in a series of violent attacks against the British presence in Palestine carried out by Jewish militants in the early 1940s.

Very Important

Faced with the death of hundreds of their own people, the British decided to suspend the emigration mandate and withdraw completely from Palestine in May 1948, concluding they could find no solution suitable to both sides. In 1947 the United Nations voted to partition the land of Palestine into separate Jewish and Arab states and make Jerusalem an international zone. Jews enthusiastically accepted the resolution while Arabs rejected it.

With the international community unable and unwilling to stop the conflict between the Jews and Arabs of Palestine, the stage was set for war.

50 yrs. of War

Chapter 16:

Israel's Beginnings (1948)

Key idea: Israel's rocky transition from British protectorate to independence created a hostile relationship with its neighbors and turbulent circumstances for Palestinians.

Why this matters to you: After this chapter you will understand the formation of the State of Israel and the origin and nature of its land feud with Palestine.

After 30 years of attempting to create a stable homeland for Muslims and Jews in Palestine, the British gave up on the task and washed their hands clean of the entire affair. In May of 1948, they packed up and left Palestine to solve its own problems.

On May 14, 1948, David Ben-Gurion, leader of the Jewish provisional government, formally declared Israel's independence. Egypt, Jordan, Syria, Lebanon, and Iraq immediately declared war against the newborn state and invaded it the very next day. To fight back, the Israeli Defense Force (IDF) and the Israeli Air Force (IAF) were formed out of the Israeli militias established during the 1936-1939 Arab revolts. This military apparatus proved successful, winning the first of many battles in the 20th century against superior Arab numbers. Major fighting ended in March 1949 and Israel signed armistice agreements with Syria, Jordan, Lebanon, and Egypt (Israel and Iraq are still technically at war to this day). Following the end of the war, Jewish holocaust survivors and inhabitants of nearby Middle Eastern countries flooded into the new nation, increasing the population from 800,000 to 2 million between 1948 and 1958.

While this signaled a victory for the fledgling Jewish state, the plight of Palestinians unfortunate enough to be living within Israel's new national borders was just beginning. Between 1948-1949 many Palestinians fled the new Jewish state with hopes they would be able to return home after Israel's defeat. Few were re-admitted after the war and most lost their homes. Furthermore, almost 800,000 Palestinians were forcibly removed from their homes within Israel during the war.

Significant autonomous pockets of Palestinians remained in regions within Israel. The first was the West Bank, an area in Israel's North that had been by Jordan since February 1949. Jordan also controlled the eastern portion of Jerusalem, including the Temple Mount. The second was the Gaza Strip, controlled by Egypt. None of these three countries accepted Palestinians into their country as refugees, as these nations had their own internal problems and could not absorb a few hundred thousand individuals. The Palestinians were left in a legal limbo status, and today the descendents of these original Palestinians number four million refugees. They still have not found a nation who will claim them and have not created a nation of their own.

Chapter 17:

The Six-Day War (1967)

Key idea: Although surrounded by hostile neighbors, Israel has been able to defend itself due to a superior military and a society trained for war.

Why this matters to you: After this chapter you will understand how Israel defends itself militarily and why this defense strategy complicates relationships between Israel and its neighbors.

Today Israel only has 7 million citizens and is surrounded by 300 million Muslims, many of whom do not acknowledge the existence of an Israeli state. Despite this fact, Israel has won four full-scale wars against the united military might of several Arab countries since gaining independence in 1948. The most impressive of these conflicts was the Six-Day War of 1967 during which Israel defeated Syria, Egypt, Jordan, and Lebanon in less than a week, tripling its land holdings in the process. How has Israel managed such military success? Because in terms of military strength, Israel is a 1350cc Suzuki Hayabusa: It has an incredibly high power-to-weight ratio.

Israeli soldiers are among the most battle-trained in the world. From age 18 Israeli men are conscripted into the Israeli Defense Force (IDF) and serve three years; women two to three years. Once this period is finished, individuals remain on reserve duty until their 40s and serve a few weeks a year. These soldiers are proficient in a number of skills, among them Krav Maga, one of the world's most brutal forms of martial arts. The IDF maintains nearly 170,000 active troops and 400,000 reservists. Israel also has the highest defense budget-to-GDP ratio in the world, spending nearly $2,300 a person. A healthy portion of this money comes from US foreign aid, worth roughly $3 billion a year - a number that has not escaped the attention of many Muslims in the Middle East.

With such a well-armed force it is no surprise that Israel handily won the Six-Day War. They gained the West Bank, the Gaza Strip, and all of the Sinai Peninsula (they later gave the Sinai Peninsula back to Egypt in the 1978 peace accords). They also occupied Syria's Golan Heights.

One unforeseen consequence of gaining lands is that the Palestinian enclaves of the West Bank and Gaza Strip belonging to Jordan and Egypt now belonged to Israel, and it remains in its hands to this day. Now that these enclaves were not controlled by fellow Muslim states, Arab countries could now blame Israelis for the plight of Palestinians without worrying that they were implicating their co-religionists in the process.

Chapter 18:

The Rise of Political Islam

Key idea: "Islamism" - the concept of Islam as the organizing point of all society - rose during the 20th century in the face of Western colonialism, Arab nationalism, and Saudi funding.

Why this matters to you: After this chapter you will understand the origins of political Islam and why it is such a unifying force across nations for hundreds of millions of people as well as what effect it has on Western nations.

In 2011 Egypt threw out its president, Hosni Mubarak, who had been in power for 29 years. At the time it was a triumph for human rights supporters, as Mubarak had used "emergency powers" to rule Egypt brutally and corruptly, ensuring that any lucrative state contracts pass through his family's bank account. But as Egypt voted for its January 2012 parliamentary elections, many Western analysts lamented that the liberal reformers who were at the forefront of the drive to remove the ex-president ultimately lost out to the Muslim Brotherhood, an international religious group which had been outlawed in Egypt for decades and is still outlawed in many Muslim countries. Why would a Muslim organization be outlawed in a Muslim country?

Because the Muslim Brotherhood is a political group that seeks to install Islam as the chief organizing principle for all of society, and it threatens the power of Muslim secularists and non-religious hard-line politicians who would try to stand in its way. The Muslim Brotherhood is among the most well-organized political Islamic groups in the world, and from this position it can fill almost any political vacuum in the Middle East, even if it is little loved by society, merely by offering a better alternative than anarchy or kleptocracy.

The group was founded in 1928 by Hassan al-Banna. Its goal is to instill the Qur'an and Sunnah as the "sole reference point for ...ordering the life of the Muslim family, individual, community ... and state." By the 1940s the number of people in this organization grew to 500,000. It sent volunteer soldiers to fight against Israel in the 1948 Arab-Israeli war.

This new political assertiveness caused fear among the Egyptian government as a possible threat to its power and Prime Minister Mahmoud an-Nukrashi Pasha officially disbanded the group in December 1948. But it lived on in semi-legal status and has now fully mobilized in Egypt. In the January 2012 elections, the Muslim Brotherhood's Freedom and Justice Party (FJP) won nearly 50% of Egypt's seats, with the hard-line Salafist Nour party coming in second. In total, the Islamist parties control two-thirds of Egypt's assembly, far more than liberal and secular parties combined.

The Muslim Brotherhood, which has received billions of dollars from Saudi Arabia (more on that in the next chapter, which discusses Middle Eastern oil), has supported many other controversial groups. Hamas - the Palestinian political party that controls the Gaza Strip and officially supports terrorism against Israel and promotes its complete destruction - is the Palestinian branch of the Muslim Brotherhood.

A less direct connection ties the Muslim Brotherhood to the Muslim Students' Association (MSA), the largest American Muslim university student association, which was founded by the Muslim Brotherhood in 1963. Its members have initiated peaceful demonstrators in the past, but they have also created controversy, such as a 2010 event at University of California-Irvine in which Israeli Ambassador Michael Oren was repeatedly interrupted by MSA students in a pre-meditated plan. Eleven MSA students were arrested, and the MSA of UC Irvine was suspended for one year.

The ability for the Muslim Brotherhood to organize itself effectively and gain political power is no longer questioned. But whether it will funnel religious sentiment in peaceful directions or destroy religious liberty remains to be seen.

?

Essential Features of the
Islamic Political System
reading material
Discuss & explain article

The Rise of Political Islam—
Muslim Brotherhood
size, & where —
infiltrated into U.S. Gvnt,
Police, etc.

Chapter 19:

The Oil Boom

Key idea: The discovery of oil in the Arab Peninsula transformed the region, made leaders obscenely rich, and created a symbiotic relationship between Middle East producers and Western consumers. Petrol dollars have also supported terrorism and extreme ideology.

Why this matters to you: After this chapter you will understand that you are intimately involved in this relationship every time you fill up at the pump.

In 1944 a petroleum geologist named Everette DeGoyler issued a report to the U.S. State Department stating that the Middle East was sitting on at least 25 billion barrels of crude oil. Unofficially, however, he estimated that the true figure was closer to 300 billion barrels. His team commented that, "The oil in this region is the greatest single prize in all history." No other single resource has fueled the Middle East economy as much as oil, nor has any other created such a strong love-hate relationship between it and Western governments.

    With an explosive growth of petroleum use across the world in the last century and parallel discovery of vast oil deposits in the Middle East, foreign petroleum companies flooded into the region. In the early days they only paid a small percentage of the oil proceeds to their host countries. Western governments supported these companies to the detriment of Middle Eastern governments, even to the point of engineering a coup d'état against the democratically elected Iranian prime minister in response to his nationalization of the oil industry. In 1990 Saddam Hussein invaded Kuwait, giving him control over a sizeable amount of global petroleum production. Whatever other reasons may have existed, there is no denying that US oil dependence was a significant motivation for the resulting Gulf War against Iraq.

To guard their own interests, Iran, Iraq, Kuwait, Saudi Arabia and Venezuela formed OPEC (Organization of Petroleum Exporting Countries) in 1960 to regulate global oil production and keep its price artificially high. While unfair to non-oil producers according to basic market economics, OPEC has used its leverage over a precious commodity to flex its muscles at various times. In 1973 the Arab members of OPEC retaliated against the US for supporting Israel during the 1973 Yom Kippur War and initiated a 5-month oil embargo. American gas prices nearly doubled in a month. While other oil discoveries around the world have weakened OPEC's monopoly somewhat, they still hold 79% of the world's crude oil reserves.

Oil has been as much of a curse as it has been a blessing to the Middle East. New York Times columnist Thomas Friedman has developed a theory that oil production has an inverse proportion to democracy. The greater the oil wealth of a nation, the less it needs the consent of its citizens to rule since it can merely bribe them into submission. The oil wealth of Saudi Arabia, Iran, Iraq and the other Gulf States has allowed them to oppress their citizens' freedoms despite heavy international sanctions and/or global marginalization.

Oil revenues also provide substantial support for highly controversial projects. Each year Saudi Arabia uses its vast oil wealth to open up fundamentalist Islamic schools across the world. According to David E. Kaplan, since 1975 Saudi Arabia has spent $70 billion to spread Wahhabi Islam, a puritanical belief system that interprets Islamic texts in the most dogmatic way possible. In addition to schools, Saudi Arabia has financed the opening of thousands of mosques and Islamic centers, which some US intelligence officials claim provides support for violent religious struggle against non-Muslims (jihad). These centers have been opened in Pakistan, Indonesia, Egypt, the Balkans, and even in the United States. Many members of the Taliban were educated in Saudi-funded Pakistani schools, as were other terrorists.

Oil, autocracy, and terrorism have created a vicious circle for the Middle East, making human rights development extremely difficult. Furthermore, since OPEC member states are unlikely to diversify their economies anytime soon, the problem appears intractable. As long as the enormous US demand for petroleum persists, these producers will always have a customer, and consequently, the United States will always be caught in this imbroglio.

This situation also results in an ironic financial trap for the US: In the last decade America spent hundreds of billions of dollars fighting terrorism in the Middle East perpetrated by graduates from Saudi Arabia schools. Yet every time an American fills up their SUV at a gas station, they fork over additional money to Saudi Arabia and its interests. To paraphrase Friedman again, the US paid for both sides of the War on Terror.

[Handwritten notes:]

founding of oil H.S. — (10)

Kuwait —

Iraq —

U.A.E. —

S.A. —

Algeria —

Lybia —

Qutar —

Oman —

Iran —

Tunesia — ?

do a chart break down of oil in M.E.

Map if possible

M.E. ties

Oil Countries?

Afghanistan

non-oil — 10

Egypt — Pakistan

Morrocco —

Jordan —

Israel —

Syria —

Lebanon —

Yemen

Yemen Rep. 75

Chapter 20:

The Palestinian Question

Key idea: The fundamental conflict between Israelis and Palestinians comes down to one question: who owns the land? Both sides claim a right to the region by ancient heritage, and both view the other side as trespassers.

Why this matters to you: After this chapter you will understand why many Israelis and Palestinians are committed to claiming the land as theirs, even to the point of death.

The struggle between the Palestinians and Jews is deeply complicated. It is an existential battle between two groups that has lasted between 60 and 4,000 years (depending on how we define these groups). Numerous attempts at peace between the two sides have failed, though they were supported and even brokered by American presidents going back to Harry Truman. On the other hand, the conflict is exceptionally easy to understand. It boils down to one simple issue: land.

Both Palestinians and Jews believe modern geographical Israel to be rightfully theirs and both claim history as their arbiter. Each group traces their proposed rights to their familial connection with Abraham. Religious Jews claim that they are the sons of Isaac, Abraham's designated heir. Meanwhile, pious Muslims say that Abraham's oldest son Ishmael was the true inheritor of Abraham's land and possession; at least this was the case that Palestinians made to the United Nations to re-obtain the homes and land from which they had been evicted following the 1948 Arab-Israeli War.

When hundreds of thousands of Palestinians fled their homes in the 1940s and 50s, many Middle Eastern nations worried that their plight would become deadly. So in the 1960s the Palestinian Liberation Organization (PLO) was formed in Egypt. The PLO was created as a political support mechanism for Palestinians to aid them in their ultimate objective of completely destroying Israel, a goal that was explicitly written on the original PLO charter. Although Yasser Arafat promised that this statement would be removed after a 1993 peace agreement, it remains to this day like a banner proclaiming the entrenched resentment Palestinians feel toward the establishment of the Israeli state.

In response to the broad human displacements out of their homes that have occurred, Palestinians claim a "right of return," meaning that first-generation refugees and their descendents have a right to the property they or their ancestors abandoned or were forced to leave during the 1948 Israeli declaration of independence and the 1967 Six-Day War. As a symbol of this sentiment, many Palestinian families keep a key to their families' home in token of their hope to one day return and reclaim what is rightfully theirs. And to this moving sentiment many Jews would swiftly respond with equal conviction that their exact purpose in coming to the region several decades ago was to claim what had been rightfully theirs for thousands of years.

Chapter 21:

Iran's Islamic Revolution

Key idea: Iran became a full-fledged theocracy in 1979 when it overthrew its dictatorial leader and replaced him with Islamic cleric Ayatollah Khomeini. Four decades later, Iran's present instability is causing some analysts to wonder if another revolution is around the corner.

Why this matters to you: After this chapter you will understand how revolutions in the Middle East spread and what role Western nations have played in these radical shifts of power.

Would you be surprised if you were told that in the 1970s, there existed a Muslim nation that fully supported women's rights, encouraged its youth to study at European universities, and whose leader deeply admired the United States? The country's citizens looked thoroughly modern, with the same sideburns and short dresses that had infested the rest of the world. For many Westerners, the surprise becomes shock when it is revealed that the country described above is Iran! What precipitated this transformation from a thoroughly modern society into a theocracy threatening nuclear war against the US and Israel?

The key to understanding this paradox is a single event in 1979: the Iranian Islamic Revolution. In the space of a few months, the former dictator Shah Mohammed Reza Pahlavi was overthrown and replaced by Ayatollah Khomeini, a religious cleric who quickly turned Iran into an Islamic theocracy. The revolution, however, was decades in the making. Shah Pahlavi slowly assumed dictatorial powers from the beginning of his reign in 1941 until 1953, when Iranians engineered a coup against him, prompting him to flee to Italy. The US and Britain overthrew his democratically elected replacement and reinstated the Shah for two reasons: (1) Iran was considered highly susceptible to falling under Soviet influence and (2) the Shah's replacement had nationalized the Iranian oil industry. The resulting legacy of these events for many Iranians has been a deep resentment against the West for its perceived interference.

But at the time, Iranians harbored deeper resentment against Shah Pahlavi, who massively curtailed any political opposition against him. He also created a cult of personality by displaying his own image across the country and showing propaganda films of himself before movies. And for his secularization policies and embrace of Israel he earned enemies from the religious establishment, most notably the outspoken cleric Ayatollah Khomeini, whom the Shah sent into exile.

Together these factors led to mass demonstrations against the Shah in 1978, culminating in a December protest in which 2 million people filled Tehran's streets, demanding the Shah's deposition and Khomeini's return. When Khomeini arrived in February 1979, he toppled the government in a week and declared Iran a theocracy.

Today the most powerful politician in Iran is the Supreme Leader, which was Khomeini until his death in 1989 and Ali Khamenei since then. He and his council vet all politicians for high office. Their responsibility is to "protect the state's Islamic character." While the current president of Iran, Mahmoud Ahmadinejad, has gained notoriety for his bizarre performances at meetings of the United Nations (choice examples include closing speeches by calling on God to bring the world to an end and hosting conferences that question the Holocaust), he is ultimately under the thumb of the Supreme Leader. This is why Ahmadinejad, who happens to hold the Supreme Leaders' favor, was declared the winner of the 2009 presidential elections despite widespread suspicion of voter fraud. The ensuing protest against these election results by millions in Iran and around the world was brutally suppressed or flatly ignored by Iranian authorities. Many Westerners see these tensions as the harbinger of an impending power shift and wonder if Iran is set for another revolution.

In addition to these internal strains, external pressures have also recently begun to mount. The UN has placed heavy international sanctions on Iran for its uranium enrichment programs that are perceived as a foil for the development of nuclear weapons, and the sanctions have crippled its economy. The population of Iran is extremely young, increasingly secular, and tired of the theocratic regime. The late political scientist Samuel P. Huntington noted that it was the only modern Islamic country in which the youth are significantly less religious than their parents. Perhaps the Iran of 10 years from now won't look all that different from its predecessor of the 1970s (minus the sideburns and bell bottoms, Insha'Allah).

Chapter 22:

A Jewish-Muslim Peace?
Yes and No

Key idea: Outside parties have negotiated peace between Israel and Palestine multiple times since 1948. While marginal progress has been made, each round of peace talks has eventually collapsed and violence between the two groups resumed.

Why this matters to you: After this chapter you will understand why peace treaties have failed between Israel and Palestine time and time again.

Over the decades of conflict between Israel and its neighbors following British withdrawal from the region, both sides began to tire of constant warfare and a new wave of diplomacy broke out in the 1970s. In 1978, Jimmy Carter managed to broker a peace agreement between Egypt and Israel.

By the terms of the agreement, Egypt became the first nation in the Middle East to formally recognize the state of Israel. In exchange, Israel returned the Sinai Peninsula to Egypt, which it had obtained in the 1967 Six-Day War (a remarkable change in geography for Israel as the peninsula constituted roughly two-thirds of its land mass, tantamount to California giving all land south of Sacramento to Mexico).

Despite the seeming advance, this call for peace angered extremists on both sides, and in 1981 a Muslim extremist assassinated Egyptian President Anwar Sadat. Following this event, diplomacy took a backseat, and in 1982 Israel invaded Southern Lebanon in retaliation to the attacks by homemade rockets Palestinian refugees were firing over the border into Israeli settlements. Israeli troops occupied this area for 18 years until their withdrawal in 2000.

There have been two key periods of Palestinian aggression against Israel since the failed peace brokerage of 1978. These periods, known as intifadas (Arabic for "shaking off", connoting a popular uprising against oppression), resulted in suicide bombings targeted to kill Israeli civilians, marking the origin of a modern terrorism technique that has become all too commonplace today.

The First Intifada took place between 1987 and 1993 as a response to Israeli occupation of Palestinian territories. In 1994 Bill Clinton brokered peace between Yasser Arafat, chairman of the Palestinian Liberation Organization (PLO), and Israeli Prime Minister Yitzhak Rabin.

But events seesawed back toward war in the Second Intifada of 2000. Following failed peace negotiations at Camp David, Israeli Prime Minister Ariel Sharon visited the Temple Mount in Israel. This area is sacred to both Jews and Muslims as it was the site of the Jewish Temple of Old Testament times and the location of the 8th century Al-Aqsa Mosque. During this visit, Sharon declared that, "the Temple Mount is in our hands and will remain in our hands. It is the holiest site in Judaism and it is the right of every Jew to visit the Temple Mount." This statement marked the beginning of five more years of riots and clashes between Palestinian civilians and the IDF.

Peace received another setback in 2006 when the PLO held a vote and elected to its parliament the political party Hamas, which calls for the utter destruction of Israel and has been labeled a terrorist organization by the United States and Europe. Israel has responded in kind by trying to isolate and marginalize them internationally. The more things change, the more they stay the same.

Why have peace treaties failed between Israel & Palestine time & time again?

The more things change, the more they seem the same.

Chapter 23:

Global Terrorism and Osama bin Laden: The Road to 9/11

Key idea: The rise of terrorism in the 20th century means that conflict has moved away from showdowns between established armies to violent acts against civilians perpetrated by fringe figures and rogue ideologues.

Why this matters to you: After this chapter you will understand the origins of modern terrorism and the conditions that allow its spread.

Terrorism has existed throughout history, but in recent times it has taken a deadly new twist. With the development of personal explosive devices in the 19th century, such as small handguns and dynamite, large-scale murders were no longer in the sole domain of armies but also available to radical ideologues and marginal groups acting on an individual basis. Anarchists such as these committed a number of high profile murders in the late 19th and early 20th century, including the assassination of US President William McKinley, Russian Tsar Alexander II, and Franz Ferdinand.

This brand of violence spread to the Middle East as well. In the 1940s members of the Egyptian Muslim Brotherhood attacked British policemen and troops located within Egypt. In the 1970s paramilitary factions of the PLO seized and eventually executed 11 Israeli athletes at the 1972 Summer Olympics in Munich. And George Habash, a Palestinian Christian, founded the paramilitary splinter group Popular Front for the Liberation of Palestine, which popularized the hijacking of airplanes as a militant tactic.

But the most infamous example of modern Middle East terrorism is without a doubt Osama bin Laden. In 1988 he founded al-Qaeda, which means "The Base" in Arabic. Born to a billionaire construction magnate in Saudi Arabia, bin Laden used his vast wealth to fund militant Islamic movements, such as the Afghan resistance to the Soviet Invasion in the 1980s. During the US-led Gulf War, he was enraged that "infidels" had inhabited the Muslim holy land. This and other events inspired him to rally Muslims to the use of violence as a means of replacing Western-dominated or Western-controlled Muslim countries with Islamic theocracies.

He based himself in Afghanistan and began coordinating terrorist activities in 1988 with attacks against US embassies based in Africa, killing hundreds. Bin Laden claimed that it was the US-Israeli alliance and the 1982 invasion of Lebanon that pushed him to plan the September 11 attacks. His plans are well-known: Nineteen Saudi Arabian men hijacked four commercial airliners and crashed them into the World Trade Center and the Pentagon, killing 3,000.

And yet that attack was only the beginning. Since 2001 there have been 18,000 reported terrorist attacks around the world perpetrated by Muslims (who themselves have sometimes claimed that Western Imperialism was a form of terrorism in their own lives). Despite bin Laden's 2011 death, these attacks continue. It is a deadly new chapter, as warfare moves away from massive armies to small groups held together by marginal ideologies and fanaticism. *False*

Chapter 24:

The Arab Spring

Key idea: Aided by social media such as Twitter and Facebook, protests and revolts swept the Middle East in 2011 due to long-term resentment against corruption, high unemployment, poverty, and human rights violations.

Why this matters to you: After this chapter you will understand how Internet-age uprisings start, and how unstable repressive regimes in the Middle East have become susceptible to decentralized networks of dissatisfied youths.

In 2011 news programs were filled with images of Arab crowds marching against corrupt governments. Protests raged across the Middle East, from Mauritania to Iraq, against the middle-aged and elderly dictators who had held on to power for decades, transferred billions of dollars from the state coffers into their private bank accounts, and stamped out any possibility of democratic reform. When the dust settled, four governments had been overthrown, major government reforms had been initiated in six nations, and minor protests had occurred in six others. Time magazine even named "The Protestor" 2011's Person of the Year. What was the event that launched this tidal wave of protests across the Arab world? As unlikely as it may seem, it all started with a 26-year-old Tunisian vegetable vendor.

On December 10, 2010, Mohamed Bouazizi set himself on fire after an argument with government officials over where he would be permitted to sell his fruits and vegetables. He had received insulting treatment from local officials and decided to make a dramatic stand against a system of endemic corruption and nepotism. This system was headed by Tunisian President Ben Ali, who had lived in obscene wealth for 23 years while the majority of Tunisians struggled to remain above the poverty line.

(1) ruler Tunisia

Sympathetic citizens rioted after his death. Soon tens of thousands gathered, spreading the word via social media like Facebook and Twitter, and swapping insulting images of Ben Ali, an unthinkable act prior to these events. Within a week, unrest had escalated to the point that 2,000 police were dispatched in an attempt to stop the riots. By January 14, Ben Ali had fled to Saudi Arabia. The rapid success of the protests proved contagious and quickly spread to other Middle East countries suffering from the same problems that had created pent-up resentment in Tunisia: chronic unemployment, few opportunities for the educated, entrenched cronyism that ensured wealth only stayed among the politically well-connected, a general lack of democracy, and outstanding human rights violations.

The coming months would see President Hosni Mubarak of Egypt resign in February after 18 days of protests, Libyan leader Muammer Gaddafi

(2) ruler Egypt

(4) leader Gaddafi Libyan

overthrown on August 23, and Yemeni President Ali Abdullah Saleh formally step down on February 27, 2012. Leaders in Jordan, Bahrain, and Lebanon have promised serious reforms to quell their citizens. Saudi Arabia even announced that women would be permitted to vote and participate in municipal elections by 2015.

The full result of the Arab Spring is still unwritten. Egypt threw out a dictator but its parliamentary election in 2012 voted in a majority of Islamists and eventually brought in President Muhammad Morsi, a member of the Muslim Brotherhood. Many of the same social problems that persisted before the uprising remain. Still, if such rapid change can come from a simple vegetable vendor, then Middle Eastern leaders may no longer feel quite so secure in their corruption.

Chapter 25:

The Middle East: The Next 20 Years

Key idea: With major social and demographic changes ahead, the Middle East is at a crossroads. Some states may evolve into free societies, while others are likely to stay mired in underdevelopment.

Why this matters to you: After this chapter you will understand that the destiny of Western countries is now intertwined more than ever with that of the Middle East. In certain ways its future is our future.

Anyone who tries to predict the events of the next 20 years in the Middle East will inevitably be wrong. The region is simply too complicated and diverse to fully understand. As we have seen, unpredicted events can trigger rapid and far-reaching social change. That being said, let's attempt to determine some likely possibilities for oncoming occurrences in the Middle East over the next two decades.

In the second decade of the 21st century, the Middle East faces tremendous challenges. An extremely high birth rate coupled with chronic unemployment means there are not enough jobs for the younger generation, and the situation is likely to get worse. According to the 2012 Freedom House Report, the Middle East consistently ranks near the bottom of the list of the world's nations in terms of education, gender equality, and human rights. Meanwhile, the Arab Spring has shown that authoritarian regimes are not safe from a revolution. Social media and global interconnectedness have loosened their grip on power, perhaps permanently.

There are two classes of authoritarian countries in the Middle East: republics and monarchies. The republics -- Syria, Algeria, Egypt, Yemen, and Tunisia -- are more likely to collapse in the next 20 years than the monarchies, which include Jordan, Morocco, Saudi Arabia, and the rest of the Arab Gulf states. The republics hold elections and although they are typically rigged, they at least give a pretense of caring about citizens' opinions. In contrast, the monarchies are ruled by a single person or family and their cult of personality ironically shields them from many of the problems experienced by republics.

    Oil wealth will also determine how fast these
countries reform. Oil-rich nations like Bahrain and
Saudi Arabia essentially bribe their citizens into
compliance. (They also allow for prestige projects,
such as the United Arab Emirates' Burj Khalifa
tower, the tallest building in the world). Their

change over time is more likely to be a slow evolution rather than a violent uprising. Oil-poor nations like Syria can only violently repress their citizens into conformity. This model has already shown its instability in Libya with Muammer Qadafi's reign and could be repeated across different countries in the coming decades.

But whatever the next stage in the Middle East, it will continue to be a dynamic area both blessed and cursed by its location at the center of the world. Whatever happens in this region will have ripple effects across the globe. Here's to hoping that the future of the Middle East is a success story and recalls its brighter moments, and not a return to the darker chapters of its history.

Excerpt from "History's Worst Dictators: A Short Guide to the Most Brutal Rulers, From Emperor Nero to Ivan the Terrible"

Chapter 4
Genghis Khan (1162-1227):
Enemy of Empires -- And Atmospheric Carbon?

In 2011 a team of ecologists from the Carnegie Institute made a startling discovery. They determined that an event between the 13th and 14th centuries caused such widespread death and destruction that millions of acres of cultivated land returned to forest, causing global carbon levels to plummet. This event was bigger than the fall of China's Ming Dynasty or even the Black Death. The team said this event was not produced by nature and actually the first, and only case of successful man-made global cooling. It was not hard to guess who was responsible: Genghis Khan and his descendants triggered 40 million deaths in this period, making him one of the bloodiest, and ironically, the greenest, dictator in history.

Through his battles and systematic slaughter, he removed 700 million tons of carbon from the atmosphere, equivalent to the amount released from one year of gasoline use today. Massive depopulation in the domains of his conquest, which covered 22 percent of the earth, resulted in the return of forests and their scrubbing of carbon from the atmosphere. While most environmentalists of today would not approve of his methods (except for some neo-Mathusians such as Sir David Attenborough, who in January 2013 lambasted humans as a 'plague on the earth'), they cannot deny that his methods achieved what carbon offsets and gas mileage standards have not. How did a tyrant whose influence was felt all the way through the earth's atmosphere rise to power and accomplish such far-reaching results?

Legend has it Temujin was born clutching a blood clot in his palm, a sign which, according to Mongol folklore, certainly foretold of his power from birth. While his reign should technically have begun when he was just nine years old, it wasn't until he was 16 that Temujin (later known as Genghis) established himself as a stealthy and cunning warrior, and warranted faith as a leader and eventually as emperor of the Mongol Empire.

Temujin was born in 1162 into the Borjigin clan, of which his father, Yesuhkei, was leader. As was the clan's tradition, Temujin was due to be married at 12 years old to a girl from the Ongirrat tribe. At the age of nine Temujin's father took him to serve the family of his bride-to-be. On the return trip home, his father was poisoned by members of a rival tribe who coaxed him into partaking in what he thought was a conciliatory drinking of fermented horse milk -- a popular beverage on the Central Asian Steppe. Hearing of his father's death, Temujin returned home but his fellow clansmen would not hear of submitting to the leadership of a child.

In the years following his father's death, it was Temujin's mother who taught him the importance of forging the right alliances. His family was ostracized and had to survive for years on their own by hunting and gathering fruit to eat. When he was 16 years old, Temujin returned to take his bride, Borte Ujin. Shortly after they wed, Borte was kidnapped by members of the Merkit tribe and given to their chieftain as a wife. This event proved to be the catalyst to launch Temujin's military career. In a short-lived alliance with Ong-Khan, an ally of his father's, and Jamuka, Temujin aligned a group of men to help him defeat the Merkits and retrieve his wife. The recovery allowed Temujin to build a support base and his popularity continued to grow. In light of his new-found power, Jamuka and Ong-Khan declared war against Temujin, a war which Temujin won.

Temujin's personal strength was in understanding the power of unity -- two heads are better than one. By the age of 20, he used this wisdom to build an army that would set out to destroy individual factions and tribes in what was soon to be his massive Mongol Empire. As he conquered, instead of chasing off the region's soldiers and killing the survivors, he instead absorbed each conquered territory into his domain, under his rule. This strategy helped him to expand the Mongol Empire quickly and efficiently, making use of all the talents, skills and abilities available in his newly acquired subjects.

He had two primary directives: dominance and unity. Any tribe that refused to unify under his rule had its leader, and sometimes the entire tribe, obliterated. The 'powerful king,' or 'Genghis Khan,' set up an information network of advisers, spies, and strategists to help him gather intelligence on rival factions planning to challenge his rule. He used that information to implement smart, effective military strategies that enabled him to build the largest contiguous empire the world had ever seen.

Part of the effectiveness of his reign is that his mission was not simply to pillage and plunder for the sake of getting more money and wives, though he had plenty of both. The goal was always to expand, subdue and rule. To do that, he used the most loyal, courageous and capable men as leaders within his empire. He used his influence and dominance to create peace throughout his empire, a period that is commonly referred to as the Pax Mongolica. Subjects were to adhere to the Khan's Yasal code, a simple system of egalitarian common law. According to its statues no one was allowed to participate in any act that would compromise the balance and integrity of the empire, whether the act was something as mundane as theft, or something subtle like polluting the water supply. The implementation of this law is an open question, but Genghis at the very least changed legal discourse in his empire.

Subjects were allowed religious freedom in his empire so those from various religions could rise high in the military and political hierarchy. Within his court Genghis had Buddhists, Muslims, and even Nestorian Christians. Genghis Khan also allowed free trade along the Silk Road and connected Southeast Asia to Central Europe. This was the route taken by Marco Polo, when from 1271 to 1295, he traveled overland from Italy to the court of Kublai Khan, Ghengis' grandson. Moral and ethical laws were set, well-known and strictly enforced. Crime was ostensibly not tolerated and if committed was swiftly and brutally punished.

Of course, Genghis Khan is not remembered today for peace and opportunity, and for good reason. To avenge his father's death, Genghis Khan wiped out the Tatar army and ordered the deaths of every Tatar male that stood less than three feet tall. If he was unable to reach peaceful trade agreements with neighboring territories -- as was the case with Khawarezmia -- the result was that Khan's 200,000-man army would be paying a visit very soon and, in Khawarezmia's case, burn down everything in its path before wiping out leadership and absorbing new subjects into the Mongol Empire.

Then there was Khan's decimation of the Middle East and Middle Eastern culture, which resulted in thousands upon thousands of deaths. In the 13th century, the Mongol army marched into Iraq and Iran and burned cultural and religious places of interest. As well, the army burned the crops and committed one of the biggest massacres in history.

Historians estimate that during his reign, Genghis Khan and his armies were responsible for some 10 million deaths, which include casualties from a series of well-orchestrated battles. His high death toll was due mainly to his conquest policy of giving young women and children to his soldiers and slaughtering the rest. In his eastern conquests he eliminated three-fourths of the population of the Iranian plateau, which it did not regain until the 20th century. In the capture of the city of Urgench, medieval historians estimate 1.2 million were killed. His immediate descendants would go on to kill another 30 million, resulting in the carbon offsetting scheme we saw at the beginning of this chapter.

The Mongol Empire was expanded to include Korea, China, the Middle East, Russia, the Caucasus and Eastern Europe. The centralized control of nearly all Eurasia allowed for stability and for trade to flourish across the region. He created one of the safest, most prosperous and culturally diverse empires in history. And the freer flow of information allowed knowledge from the classical period to enter European universities, suggesting that his influence partially influenced the beginning of the European Renaissance.

Similar to many of the dictators under consideration in this book, he was capable of surprisingly peaceful action when brutally was not necessary

[End of Excerpt] If you enjoy this portion of 'History's Worst Dictators,' you can grab your copy on Amazon.com.

Other Books in This Series, Available on Amazon.com

1) History's Worst Dictators: A Short Guide to the Most Brutal Rulers From Emperor Nero to Ivan the Terrible, by Michael Rank

Nasty, brutish, and short.

That is the way English philosopher Thomas Hobbes described the natural state of mankind and the condition into which humans inevitably fall without a strong, central authority. However, Hobbes would likely agree that living under a brutal dictator could lead to violent death we well. He would know -- he lived a century after the bloody reign of Henry VIII, 150 years after Spanish conquistadors witnessed Montezuma II offering up thousands of human sacrifices, and four centuries after Genghis Khan rode throughout Eurasia, leaving enough death and destruction behind him to depopulate major parts of the globe.

This exciting new book from historian Michael Rank looks at the lives and times of the worst dictators in history. You will learn about their reigns and violent actions, such as...

- Emperor Nero's murder of family members, suspected arson of Rome, and widespread execution of religious minorities, which caused many early Christians to believe that he was the Antichrist

- Herod the Great's use of crowd slaughter, family killings, and even infanticide to hold on to his rule

- Genghis Khan's military conquests that killed tens of millions and caused millions more to flee their homes in fear, resulting in forests reclaiming abandoned farmland and carbon levels plummeting, actually creating man-made global cooling

- Vlad the Impaler (also known as Vlad Dracul, the namesake of the vampire) and his use of impalement to kill more than 20,000 victims, even causing a superior army turn around and avoid fighting him when they witnessed his carnage

These four leaders and six others from ancient, medieval, and early modern history fill this book. Learn about how they earned their reputation as the worst dictators in history and why they are so infamous in popular culture today.

2) History's Most Insane Rulers: Lunatics, Eccentrics, and Megalomaniacs From Emperor Caligula to Kim Jong Il

Few mixtures are as toxic as absolute power and mental instability. When nothing stands between a leader's whims and carrying them out, all sorts of bizarre outcomes are possible. Whether it is Ottoman Sultan Ibrahim I practicing archery on his palace servants and commissioning his advisers to find the fattest woman in the Empire as his wife or Turkmenistan President Turkmenbashi renaming the days of the week after himself and constructing an 80-foot golden statue that revolves to always face the sun, crazy leaders have plagued society for millenia.

This book will look at the lives of the ten most mentally unbalanced figures in history. Some suffered from genetic disorders that led to schizophrenia, such as French King Charles VI, who thought he was made of glass. Others believed themselves to be God's representatives on earth and wrote religious writings that they guaranteed to the reader would get them into heaven. Whatever their background, these rulers show that dynastic politics made sure that a rightful heir always got on the throne – despite their completely insane condition – and that power can destroy a mind worse than any mental illness.

3) Wonder is a Verb: An Uncommon Crash Course in the Art of Philosophical Thinking. By Thomas Swanson, 2013.

Philosophical thinking is a skill that is sadly neglected, and sometimes even scorned, in popular culture. Medieval Philosophy expert Thomas Swanson paints a contrary picture of what philosophical thinking is in this uncommon book sharing how he believes the quest of philosophy really started; in wonder: in the hearts of curious men and women in awe of a wonderful world. After reading this book you will:

1. Have much a deeper appreciation of those mysterious creatures so common in life yet ofte overlooked: questions, thoughts, and answers.

2. Possess a little-known antidote to boredom and lack of curiosity.

3. Be conversant with some of the earliest and most famous philosophers' views on the nature of our world, following them as the skill of philosophical thinking and understanding progresses through history, from one thinker to the next.

Recommended Reading

These are books I consider the best for serving as an introduction to Middle East history for those with little background knowledge and also for their scholarly polish. Some of the books are highly entertaining and others are a bit dry, but they are worth the read for anyone who wants to become well-informed on this part of the world. I have ranked the books from the most ancient time period to the most recent.

1) Daniel Snell. Life in the Ancient Near East, 3100-332 B.C.E. (Yale University Press, 1998)

2) Simon Baker. Ancient Rome: The Rise and Fall of an Empire (BBC Books, 2007)

3) Martin Lings. Muhammad: His Life Based on the Earliest Sources (Inner Traditions, 2006)

4) Fred Donner. Muhammad and the Believers: At the Origins of Islam (Belknap Press, 2012)

5) Michael Sells. Approaching the Qur'an: The Early Revelations (White Cloud Press, 2007)

6) Hugh Kennedy. When Baghdad Ruled the Muslim World: The Rise and Fall of Islam's Greatest Dynasty (Da Capo Press, 2006)

7) Thomas Madden. The New Concise History of the Crusades (Rowman & Littlefield Publishers, 2005)

8) Richard Fletcher. Moorish Spain (University of California Press, 2006)

9) Jack Weatherford. Genghis Khan and the Making of the Modern World (Broadway, 2005)

10) Thomas Friedman. From Beirut to Jerusalem (Picador, revised and updated; 2012)

About the Author

Michael Rank is a doctoral candidate in Middle East history. He has studied Turkish, Arabic, Persian, and Armenian, but can still pull out a Midwestern accent if need be. He also worked as a journalist in Istanbul for nearly a decade and reported on religion and human rights.

He is the author of the #1 Amazon best-seller "From Muhammed to Burj Khalifa: A Crash Course in 2,000 Years of Middle East History," and "History's Worst Dictators: A Short Guide to the Most Brutal Leaders, From Emperor Nero to Ivan the Terrible."

Connect With Michael

I hope you have enjoyed this book and learned much about the history of the Middle East.

But whether you loved it or didn't, please leave a review on the book's Amazon.com page. And if you happened to like the book, feel free to click on the "Like" button.

You can also connect with me on my Facebook page and on Twitter at @michaelrank5mc. I love to connect with readers, and I am always giving away free copies of my other books.

If you are interested in getting more info about the Middle East and other parts of the world, please check out the blog posts and podcasts at my website
http://fiveminutecourses.com

Made in the USA
San Bernardino, CA
28 February 2014